The
Trilobite®
Micro-Survival Kit

The Worlds BEST 5-Ounce Survival Kit

All contents in this booklet are unique, and are copyrighted. The contents may be cited in review articles, but may not be copied and resold. The ideas of putting a survival kit inside a paracord housing is not exactly proprietary, but the contents & arrangements of such items are.

Individuals are encouraged to make their own Trilobites, or to purchase one of our Trilobites, and personalize it.

The author of this work can assume no liability for the use or misuse of any of the components mentioned here. I cannot take responsibility for the saving of or loss of a life.

Creating a Trilobite® – Survival You Can Wear

Survival experts agree – in order to survive you need Attitude; Knowledge (including skills); & Equipment. And it is also true that the more you have of skills, attitude, & knowledge, the less 'stuff' you will need. But the 'stuff' is still important.

Having been an outdoorsman all of my life, traipsing around the Alpine lakes of the Bitterroot-Selway Wilderness in western Montana & northern Idaho, to the high mountain deserts of southern Utah, I have found that prior preparation is vital. On more than one occasion I have found myself 'turned around,' & wishing that I had prepared better than I did. Sure, there were times that I did have a survival kit with me, and this was helpful. But rarely did I use even 20% of the five pounds of items that it consisted of. And during my routine hikes, I didn't even touch this 'dead weight' if I carried it at all. The chance of my using it wasn't worth either the expense or the weight of carrying it along.

It wasn't until about 2010, that I was introduced to a fad – paracord bracelets. Not being into fads myself, I bought one only for the thought of having 8' of paracord with me all the time. I liked the idea.

Then I began to wonder if I could put a few additional items into the bracelet, woven in, thus making it even more beneficial to me in my traipsing in the outdoors. So, bit by bit, piece by piece, I began to add items that I considered to be of most importance in a survival situation. Having worked in a wilderness survival program, I knew what I could use, what was lightweight, & what was needed to sustain life.

Thus, the Trilobite was born. It is so named because of the shape of the Wild-Bite. I thought that it looked like a Trilobite, one of those ancient animals whose fossil can be found in west central Utah. Through experimentation, experience, & trial & error the Trilobite Survival Kit came into existence.

We have since branched out into production of various ways to carry a trilobite, & have created a Trilobite for young children as well as youth. It is our hope that the Trilobite will become a household name, and that every man, woman, & child will have a Trilobite in their home. It is my conviction that the Trilobite may indeed be a means, someday, of saving lives, for which purpose it has been created.

Table of Contents

Introduction
What's in Your Kit (What did the Trilobite have for Dinner?)

Chapter One
Survival Priorities: First Things First

Chapter Two
Using Your Trilobite to Help Provide Emergency First Aid

Chapter Three
Using Your Trilobite to Build a Shelter

Chapter Four
Using Your Trilobite to Build a Fire

Chapter Five
Using Your Trilobite to Obtain & Carry Water

Chapter Six
Using Your Trilobite to be Rescued

Chapter Seven
Using Your Trilobite to Procure Food

Summary
The Trilobite Family Tree

Introduction
What did the Trilobite have for Dinner?

What is in your Trilobite? Because really, it's the stuff inside that counts. What is on the outside is cool looking, but in a survival situation, looks really don't matter. Performance, and outcome, do.

There are three options as far as a Trilobite goes. You can **purchase one ready-made** from me. If you have done this, all of the items are already wrapped up and ready to go. You will see a few of the items, but generally, most of the kit is 'buried' inside of the paracord.

You can **purchase a Trilobite Do-It-Yourself Kit**. In this situation, all of the items needed for the Trilobite Micro-Survival Kit are sent to you, disassembled, and you put them together. This is a good way to go. You will know what you have and how it all fits together.

Lastly, **you can put your own micro-survival kit together**. I choose to use paracord to house my items. Some folks choose an Altoids tin. Still others use a small bag. Whatever it is that you decide, it will be yours - personalized. Without the unique and proprietary design, it is not a Trilobite, but it will still be extremely useful, and hopefully lifesaving.

But, the very important thing is for YOU to know what the Trilobite had for dinner. YOU need to know WHAT is inside the Trilobite, and how to use these items. If you are not aware of what is inside, you will have basically five ounces of useless items on your hand, and when the time comes to use it, you're survival will depend more upon luck than knowledge or skill.

Why Trilobite?

We call our micro-survival kits Trilobites. Why? Because they look like a Trilobite, a small prehistoric aquatic critter. Fossils of the Trilobite can be found in a desert not far from where we live. We have been out to the fossil beds and have been able to come home with the calcified remains of these prehistoric creatures.

After our initial Trilobite, we developed some additional ways of carrying the survival items around. This led to the *family* of Trilobites. A more detailed description of the various kits can be found in Chapter Seven. However, for practical purposes, we have found that the original Trilobite is the most versatile, and is the one which we sell the most.

The purpose of this chapter is to list & detail the items as well as possible uses for each item, which are found in the Trilobite. So, THESE are what the Trilobite ate!!!

550 Parachute Cord
Shelter; First aid; Fishing line; Bow drill fire; Snares; Thread; Rope; Tourniquet; Backpack straps; Securing gear; Boot laces; Friction saw + hundreds of more uses

Hacksaw Knife
Cutting; Sawing; Shelter; First Aid; Food Preparation; Fire Preparation; Sharpening; Weaponry; etc.

Wire
Cutting; Sawing; Shelter; First Aid; Food Preparation; Fire Preparation; Sharpening; Weaponry; etc.

Needle (& Thread)
First Aid (slivers, sutures); Equipment repair; Clothing repair; Compass (if magnetized); Awl; Tie off a water bag; etc.

Bright Ribbon
Communication; Location marking

Whistle
Attract attention; Scare wild animals

Safety Pin

Secure clothing; Fishing; Sliver removal; Repair clothing; Making a sling; Improvised compass; Suture; Puncture finger or toenail (when hot) to relieve pressure; Pop blisters; Repair eyeglasses; Replace a zipper pull; Secure bandages; Replace missing buttons; Push-pin; Make a finger splint; Wound closure; Make a sling by pinning shirt sleeve to the shirt; Making traps; Make a blanket into a sleeping bag

Flashlight

Light source; Signaling; Psychological stabilizer

Fishhook

Fishing; Traps; Snare Birds; Retrieve items out of reach; Support a cooking utensil

Fishing Line

Fishing; Snares; Wounds; Lashing; Securing Gear; Weapons

Jute

Tinder; Shelter; Binding

Metal Match

Fire

Water Container (Glove)
Hold water; Flotation device; Sling shot; Tourniquet

Compass
Determine direction

Key Ring/Carabineer
Hold implements; Binding

Magnifying Glass
Fire; First aid; Improve vision

Finish Nails
Spears; Arrows; Shelter; Bent nail for snare

Razor Blade
Cutting; First aid; Detail work

Lighter (you provide)
Fire; Psychological comfort

Magnesium Bar
Fire

Mora Knife

Cutting; Sawing; Shelter; First Aid; Food Preparation;
Fire Preparation

Dental Floss

Binding; Thread; First aid; Cleaning teeth; Lashing;
Clothes line; Binding for snow glasses; Fishing Line;
String up for a clothes or other line; Hang food; stitch a
wound; Make a net; Construction of a snare; Cordage
for bow drill; Mend clothing; Makeshift shoelaces;
Shelter construction; Wrap the ends of a rope; Fire
starting; Secure hair (if hair is long); Lashing a knife or
scissors to a stick; delivery of babies; Affixing gear;
Cutting food & similar products; Securing pant legs;
Repairing shoes; Snow shoe bindings; Handcuffs;
Support garden vines; Fixing eye glasses; Pull a loose
tooth

Chapter One: Survival Priorities
First Things First

Success: Attitude; Skills (Knowledge); Tools

Scenario: You go on a day-hike, and anticipate a fun, five-hour hike into the back country. You go with your wife, but don't let anyone else know specifically what you are doing or where you're going. You look forward to time away from the hustle and bustle of 'civilization.'

Two hours into your hike, you start thinking that it may be wise to turn around. You're not is as good a shape as you used to be. Your wife is just plain tuckered out, though she suffers in silence and doesn't complain. The 'fun' is still present, though wearing off. Then, in the distance, you hear it. Rolling thunder.

But, it's miles away and the desert canyon that you're in is bone dry and hasn't seen a drop of water in what appears to be decades! Then the rain starts to come. But it's only a light rain. This doesn't worry you. In fact, it's almost a welcome relief. You sit down on a boulder in the dry stream bed to take a break prior to heading back. Your wife does the same. You both remove your day packs to cool off, and 'zone out.'

Neither of you registers the sound that starts far off as a low rumble. In fact, it sort of blends in with the rest of the sounds, and is even somewhat comforting.

But then, what was a low rumble is almost in an instant a loud roar. You break from your daze to look up the canyon, and though you can't see anything yet, you suddenly have a tight feeling in your chest, and a million butterflies in your stomach! You rouse your wife from her rest and in an almost panicked voice tell her to grab her pack and run after you.

So, there you are – running down the canyon you just minutes before had lazily & slowly hiked up. But this time, you don't feel the burning in your legs, or the sweat above your brows. You don't feel the pounding of your heart. You don't feel the water starting to lap at your ankles, but you do quickly notice that within 30 seconds it has risen to your knees.

It hits you – you're in a flash flood!

There begins to be debris shoot past you, and then you are knocked down. You lose your grip on your pack, and as you try to grab it, you go under. You soon realize that it is all you can do to get your head above water and keep it there, so in your mind you think – 'I'll retrieve it further downstream. Why should I carry it anyway?'

Then you panic. You look for your wife, and find that she is struggling as well. You holler to her, and she barely hears you. 'Drop your pack,' you say, 'and come towards me.' She obeys, and soon the two of you are more floating downstream than hiking. You watch the walls of the cliff pass by, much faster than if you had been hiking, so there is a brief moment of feeling like you're making good progress.

Then your wife attempts to stand up and screams out in pain. She cannot place any weight on her ankle. You rush to her and attempt to put her on your back in a piggy-back fashion. But all that this does is push you under, with the current, the floaties, and your lack of continued strength. You realize that you need to get out of the water, so you look around, and finally see a place that you think you can make it to dry ground. You point this out to your wife, and both of you start to make your way to the side of this previously beautiful, previously dry, canyon. By pure luck, but mostly divine intervention, you make it. But as you reach up to pull yourself out of the water, your hand slips. You look up at the rock and wonder why the hand-hold didn't work as you had anticipated. There is a strange color to it. But this only registers, and you don't have time to think about it. So, you reach up again, and realize all too quickly that your hand is the source of this strange color. Somewhere along the way, a huge gash has been inflicted upon your hand, and the palm of your hand from your thumb to nearly the wrist has been laid bare. The strange color is the blood that is coming from your hand. Due to the excitement of your adventure, & probably the chilliness of the water, you haven't yet noticed the pain.

So, plans change. You call your wife to you and get her up to dry ground, then she turns around and with your good hand, you grab her good hand, and are helped up by her.

And, there you sit, with rushing water inches away, no back packs, no clothes except for what you are wearing, no water bottles, no matches, no knives. And darkness coming on!

Neither of you say much for a few minutes, and then you notice that, nearly as quickly as it began, the water & noise now begin to subside. Within minutes what used to be a boiling torrent of dirt, water, & debris is now a small stream. And if neither of you had been hurt, you could hike back now, and probably get your injuries looked after in a matter of hours. But as it was, neither of you are in any position to move. And worse, nobody knows where you are!

But, first things first. And that is – you prepare yourself to not get help from anyone else, and to stay the night.

Duties (& limitations) of a Trilobite

Your Trilobite is like an insurance policy. You spend money for it, but hope that you never have to use it. If you do need it, however, you want to know that it's there and you want to know how to use it.

BUT, having a Trilobite is only one of THREE major components of survival. And actually, it is only a PART of one of THREE major components of survival. However, in my estimation it is a very necessary part. As I read about incidents of disaster, and how it is understood that some folks died, I have come to the conclusion that it is very likely indeed that some lives could have been spared if the person in crisis had a Trilobite & knew how to use it.

Your Trilobite is designed to help you get through the first hours & days of a crisis. The components included within the Trilobite are included based upon research, feasibility, weight, & usefulness.

This booklet will explore the major areas that your Trilobite can be of assistance to you in.

Chapter Two: Using Your Trilobite
to Help Provide Emergency First Aid

So, here you sit. Stranded about five miles from your vehicle, with nobody knowing where you are, a large gash on your hand that requires immediate attention, a badly sprained or broken ankle for your wife, night coming on soon, with no equipment, as it was all swept away.

But wait – you remember that little neck piece that you are wearing. It is a Knife-Bite. A few years ago your wife came across the Knife-Bite at a preparedness expo. This 'micro' survival kit caught her eye, and she purchased two. One for her and one to 'gift' to you on Father's Day.

You look over at her, and realize that she too has her Knife-Bite draped around her neck. Because you decided to wear them around your neck, you didn't lose them with the rest of your washed-away belongings. What a great idea to always have the Trilobite on your own person.

You quickly make an assessment of your situation, and apart from the small bumps & bruises that you have after the ordeal, the two major problems seem to be your cut and your wife's ankle.

Triaging, you determine, and confirm it with your wife, that the cut on your hand is the most pressing of the two. You are still losing blood, and it needs to be stopped.

Using your knife, you cut off part of one of your long sleeves on your shirt and apply direct pressure to the wound. Using some of the 25 feet of paracord wrapped around your knife sheath, you secure your sleeve bandage to the wound, thus freeing you up to work on other issues.

You take the latex glove from your micro kit and, using the other sleeve, construct a sleeve for the glove to fit in to, with the safety pin from your Knife-Bite being used to close up one end of the sleeve. Then you head down to the once-roaring creek to gather some water. Using part of your sleeve as a pre-filter, you fill the glove with about a gallon of water, and return up the hill about 20 yards to your wife. Your hope is to use the water to rinse the wound.

Meanwhile, your wife takes her Knife-Bite apart, and is able to find about three inches of her jute twine that is dry. Picking it apart, she makes tinder out of it and then attempts to light it with the lighter. After about five attempts to get a spark, she remembers that a wet lighter will not ignite. But this is only a temporary setback. She simply pull out the hacksaw knife and metal match and with just a few tries, is able to produce huge sparks, one of which lands in the jute tinder bundle and immediately lights. The small dry wood that has been gathered is then placed on the jute twine, and soon a fire is going.

The razor blade is then placed in the fire and sterilized, in order that the ragged skin on the cut on your hand can be trimmed out.

You consider sewing the cut on your hand with the needle and either the dental floss or a small string from the paracord. However, you decide against this, hoping that professional medical care will be obtained within 12 hours or so. You also consider that you could use a straightened-out fish hook.

You then look at your wife's ankle, and determine that if you are to get out of the situation, you must be the one to walk. Even with improvised crutches, it is a sure bet that she won't be able to make it out.

You are glad that you have a flashlight, small though it is. It will make the night much more easy in terms of being able to continue your first aid, should the need arise.

With what time is left of the sunlight, you gather small pieces of wood, and your wife, who has two good hands, is able to whittle these pieces into some splint pieces, which helps her to keep her ankle from bending.

Chapter Three:
Using Your Trilobite to Build a Shelter

Something More Than the Clothes on Your Back!

With a fire going, the emergency medical conditions being taken care of, and a rough plan for the morning, you set about making a shelter. Looking around you are blessed to find a tree that is high enough from future floods that has been blown over. It is stable, sturdy, and has branches on it. You clear an entrance hole by breaking some of the branches off of it, and then set about clearing out a sleeping space for two.

You step back after a half hour's worth of work, and realize that there is a slight gap in it that allows the wind to come in. You cut down a few larger branches from another tree, set them up against the downed tree, and tie them there with part of your paracord. You then gather the smaller branches and make the wall of your shelter without gaps. You do consider using your wire or your jute twine, but then realize that the jute is better used for other purposes, and the wire will best be used as a handle for the tin can that you just found. You plan on boiling water in the tin can, and will use the wire as a handle.

But as for shelter, you realize that when you go out tomorrow, and your wife stays, she will need protection from the wind as well as the sun and possible rain. You do your best to gather additional materials to put on the shelter.

Some Shelter Principles & Concepts
Adapt & Improvise

If you are around man-made items and can use them, do so. Use plastic, a tarp, an old watering trough, the hood of a vehicle, etc. Whatever you can use to shield yourself from the elements is great. Let your imagination run wild. It's time to be like a child again. Pretend. Look around you. If you were to pretend, what would you use to cover yourself? Get creative. It's OK. If you can find something to cut down on the number of calories you use, do it!

Lashings

It is wise to, right now, learn how to do some basic lashings. Learn how to tie two sticks together perpendicular to each other. Can you make it strong with a minimum of amount of rope being used? Can you use your knife to help with cutting joints, to make the lashings more secure? Conserve both calories and rope as much as you can.

Search the Internet for 'Lashings.' Go to Images to see some good examples.

Chapter Four:
Using Your Trilobite to Build a Fire

Having already addressed the lighting of a fire in the story, this chapter will explore various other principles in fire building as it relates to your Trilobite.

Many Ways to Light a Fire

There are dozens of ways to start a fire. The most simple are those ways known to most folks – lighters & matches. Given a little thought, a number of other 'common methods' come to mind. Bow-drill fire (friction of wood on wood), flint & steel, metal match (mischmetal, often confused with flint & steel), & a magnifying glass. A bit more thought leads to thinking of some rather unconventional ways: using a battery & wire (either 9 volt and steel wool, or a car battery and larger wire), & the parabolic reflector inside most flashlights

Lighters – The Way to Go

Well, when it comes to survival, I'm not one to take the *creative* way at the expense of calories or common sense! MOST of the Trilobites that we make can have a regular lighter taped to them. Do it! This is the best way to make a fire. Using Duct Tape (a bright color is good, so that you can find your Trilobite if you leave it laying around), make about five or six wraps around the lighter & Trilobite. This way, you will have *easily* at your disposal the ability to make fire (used for warmth, comfort, cooking, protection, soothing psychology). The Wrist-Bite is the only one of the Trilobite family that I have not yet figured out how to attach a lighter without it being in the way. Otherwise, get on it now. Get the lighter.

A word to the wise – get a lighter that is see-through. You'll want to know how much fluid you have. Also, if you have a fall you'll be able to tell right away if any of your fluid is leaking.

And a second word to the wise – a lighter that is submerged will NOT light, or even spark, for a few hours. Don't get rid of your lighter if it doesn't light after getting wet. Let it dry out, be patient, and you will find that it will again work.

Other Fire-Starting Methods
BUT, if you are in a position where you cannot use your lighter or if you don't have a lighter, you will want to know how to start a fire using other methods.

Matches

I used to include in all of the kits two strike-anywhere matches. This is fine & good, but I went away from including matches for three reasons. One is age. As they age, they deteriorate (I guess this is true with most things, including our body). Two, the sharp ends tended to poke little teeny holes in the water containers that are included in the kits, and this wasn't good. And third, there are other methods that are just as effective, but that last longer, such as a ...

Metal Match

A metal match is a piece of rare-earth metal that, when scraped by another piece of metal, gives off sparks. There are various components of different types of metals in a metal match, but generally the combination is known as Ferrocerium. The sparks that are produced when this metal is scraped are in excess of 3,000 degrees!!! Just get a spark on you, and you will now right away that it's hot!

Most Ferrocerium Firesteel produced today contains a compound of cerium, lanthanum, neodymium, praseodymium, iron, and magnesium. They come in all shapes & sizes. The one that you receive in the Trilobites are about 2 inches long and quite small in diameter. This is to make them not only lightweight, but also because of their size. The kit can be made more portable with a smaller sized rod.

Nevertheless, you ought not get discouraged due to size. Even with the small size of the metal match, you will still be able make dozens of fires.

To make a fire with your metal match, take your jute twine, cut about 3 inches off of it, strip it apart, make a ball of it between your palms, then take the hacksaw knife included in your kit and scrape quickly the metal match. Sparks will fly. Just get them to fly into the tinder made by the jute twine. If you have prepared additional tinder & kindling well, you will soon have a nice fire!

Bow-Drill

This is something that beginners would do well to practice well in advance of needing it.

You will need about three feet of your Paracord, a bow on which to tie the paracord, a fireboard, a spindle, a palm rock (or similar item that can hold the top part of your spindle), some tinder (jute twine), & your knife. Using these components, you can start a bow-drill fire. This booklet on Trilobites is not the place for an in-depth instruction on how to build and use a bow-drill set, but we do have a booklet for sale that does address this in-depth. I would encourage you to purchase this booklet, then build your own set, and practice with it.

Hand Drill

A hand drill operates on the very same principle as a bow drill, except that rather than use a bow as the object to turn a spindle, your hands are what is used. It takes much more practice, as well as tougher hands.

Again, a booklet has been put together by Dyehard Survival which instructs a person on how to make and use a hand drill.

Magnifying Glass

Capturing and focusing the energy of the sun is an extremely fast way of making a fire. This is easy to do, but again, it does require practice.

A magnifying glass is included with both our Knife-Bite and Neck-Bite kits. You may choose to add a magnifying glass to your other kits.

I ought to add that a Fresnel Lens also works well. I have one about the size of a credit card, and it fits into my wallet very well. It can be bent slightly and still retain the qualities needed to work.

Wire

Using some wire, you can short out a battery and get a spark. I have found the most success in using a 9V battery, though a 1.5V AA battery will also work.

Our Neck-Bite kit includes a Nebo flashlight that is powered by a AA battery.

Magnesium Bar

A Magnesium Bar is simply a metal match that is glued onto some magnesium. The supplied hacksaw blade is used to scrape about a dime's worth of Magnesium into a pile, then scraping the metal match with the hacksaw blade, creating sparks. When the spark his the magnesium, it bursts into flames. Buring hot, but not long, you must have tinder ready to put on the fire.

In my estimation, this is the most reliable and sure-fire (no pun intended) way of making a fire. It is naturally waterproof, doesn't seem to deteriorate with age, is large enough to find when you need it, and yet small and light enough to carry around with you. It can be soaked for hours, pulled out, dried out briefly, and then promptly used.

Get one and practice!

This comes with the Neck-Bite.

Chapter Five:
Using Your Trilobite to Obtain & Carry Water

Story

So, there you sit, with your sleeve filled with the waterproof glove and water. You take the metal can which your wife found and clean it out as best as you can. It is not rusty, but just dirty. You then fill it with water, taken from your glove, and boil it. You use this disinfected water to clean out your wound, and when it cools, to drink.

You are a Walking Water Balloon!

Water! An essential element for all life (as we know it)!

Did you know that about 80% of a baby body (in the womb) is water! Wow. That's a lot.

At birth this is down about 5%, to about 75%, and then drops to about 65% in young adults. A 'mature' person (over 60 – let's home we are mature by then) is down to about 50% water.

But still, let's face it – being half water is still a LOT of water! No wonder water is so very important to life. Even before we knew the above stats, we did know that towns, settlements, & cities were all centered around the availability of water. Even today, with our well-drilling technology & water-carrying pipes, we still locate around great rivers & small streams & bubbling brooks & friendly fountains. Water is important!

Food vs. Water

When a person is in 'survival' mode, having water is MUCH more important than any type of food. In fact, having worked in hospice now for over a decade, I can tell you that I have seen people live for 40 days (literally) without food, but never more than THREE days without water (& not be totally delirious). And when 'surviving,' it is vital to remember that you should NOT take food in without taking water in! You see, it takes water to digest any food you eat. And if you have food in your tummy, but not water, you're in for trouble.

If you ever get lost, the very first thing to do is sit down, and compose yourself. Get your head on straight, and your emotions in check. THEN, help your rescuers find you (discussed in a later chapter). But ALWAYS, from minute one of activity when you're lost, be on the look out for water.

Your Water Container

Your survival kit is supplied with a water container (you're seen one before – a latex glove). Use this to carry water with you. Only put safe drinking water in it. And use the glove (or condom, supplied in some kits) as the waterproof part of the entire water system.

I recommend that you take a long sleeve off of one of your shirts, or use part of a pants leg, or improvise your shirt, backpack, etc, to help strengthen and support the glove. Example – rip your long sleeve off at the shoulder, tie one end closed (or close it with a safety pin, etc) insert the glove into the sleeve, and fill the glove up with water. This will help to protect the glove, but it will also give the glove some form, allowing the glove to be carried without as much fear of being broken.

There are a few other items that can be utilized in procuring & making water safe.

> 550 Parachute Cord: using one of the nails or a stick, find a weeping wall. Cut a piece of paracord about 2' long, and on one end, poke the nail through the paracord and into the wall. Make sure that the Paracord is touching the wall where the nail goes through it. Soon, the paracord should be soaked, and water will start to drip off the hanging end. Put your glove or other container below this drip to catch the water.

Hacksaw Knife: use to help carve out a digging stick to use in digging in dry stream beds, or, as a last resort, to make a solar still.

Wire: You can use this in place of the nail, if needed.

Needle (& Thread): Again, use this in place of the nail.

Safety Pin: Use in place of the nail, or use to close one end of the water carrier

Jute: You can use this instead of paracord.

Metal Match: Use this to start a fire to purify water.

Magnifying Glass: use to start a fire to purify water.

Finish Nails: Secure paracord to a weeping wall.

Shirt: Though not part of your Trilobite, you will probably have a shirt. Use your shirt, or bandana, or any type of porous material to strain the water prior to disinfecting it.

Chapter Six:
Using Your Trilobite to be Rescued

Story

After a restless night with very little sleep, and still an hour before sunrise, but with light creeping into the picture, you kiss your wife goodbye, and head out. Your car is about five miles away, and you plan on being there in a little less than two hours, if all goes well, given that you walk about three miles an hour.

But before you go, you have done a little more hunting, and found a ripped up orange tarp with the grommets ripped out of it. You find an open spot in the terrain, and you use some of your small paracord strings to tie the tarp out between pieces of sage brush. Using small rock about 1" in diameter, you tie around the tarp and the sage, making it so that any aircraft flying overhead can see the tarp. It is a bit windy, so without being tied down, the tarp would blow away. But in this case the wind does make the tarp flap, and any type of movement is good.

You also set up a series of three fires near your wife, about ten feet apart. They are not lit, but are ready to light from her fire, in case she hears an airplane flying overhead. She can light these three fires and put on the green sagebrush in order to make as much smoke as possible. It just so happens that you also found an old piece of tire, and you were able to get some small pieces of tread off of the tire, which you also put by the fires. Black smoke is easier to see during the day, and the tires will burn black.

You also take the surveyors tape that is in the Knife-Bite and tie it up on various bushes in order to attract attention from hikers, mostly, as it is doubtful that it would be seen from an aircraft.

Your wife knows that if she is to spend another night in the wilds, to also use her light to flash movement or sound. If it is a rescue party, they will come to her with the attention this creates. If it is a wild animal, they will tend to shy away.

And of course, the whistle is used to attract attention. It takes much less energy to blow on a whistle than it does to scream or yell, and the pitch it creates is known to carry a lot further than human voice.

Lastly, you shine up the blade of your wife's knife, knowing that although it is very small, the reflection from the sun off of the blade may indeed do enough to attract attention from a passerby or an aircraft.

Chapter Seven:
Using Your Trilobite to Procure Food

Story

 You are hungry as you set out. Your wife is hungry. But you realize that you will be able to call on reserves to save you and carry you through to your vehicle. Though our modern society has conditioned us to have three square meals a day, it is true that our ancestors didn't get close to as much food as you and I get. And they lived.

 You will live to, and without food. The other items are much more important than food.

 BUT, food is still important. It is good to have food, though it's not good to expend more calories obtaining food than it is in getting the food you need.

 Using some of your paracord, wire, knife, fishhook, and dental floss, you set up two traps for your wife. One is a Piute deadfall, whilst the other is a Figure Four. It is hoped that by so doing, your wife will at least be able to get some sort of food to eat whilst waiting for the rescue team to come. Snakes, birds, & rats are among the animals that you may reasonably expect to capture, if anything is captured at all.

 Having already learned how to make the traps, you didn't spend a lot of time or energy on them.

(NOTE: I also publish a booklet on various types of traps and how to make them.)

Food Comes in All Shapes & Sizes

Whilst calories are often seen in our modern society as a 'problem,' in the wilderness calories are energy. Calories means life. And these calories come from food.

Indeed, I have seen & have known some individuals who have live for *40 days* without eating anything. But, these are individuals who are on hospice, and who just lay in bed, whilst the only exercise they get are breathing, smiling, thinking, sleeping, & occasionally jumping to conclusions! They don't need much food.

But, in a survival situation, food is needed to keep on going. And in order to get food, creativity, ingenuity, perseverance, & some know-how & tools are necessary. I have tried to include in the Trilobite some of the most useful, lightweight items that can be used for the procurement of food.

Chapter Eight:
The Trilobite Family Tree

Wild-Bite

- Carried whilst hanging from your belt loop, pack, car mirror, neck, or wherever else you want, by using a carabineer, spring hook, additional paracord, snap hook, etc.
- Includes 12+' of paracord, 4" hacksaw knife, 4' wire, needle, 3 safety pins, 6' of alerting ribbon, 3 fish hooks, 10' of fishing line, 4' of jute twine tinder, metal match, latex water container, 3 nails, 4' dental floss, a razor blade, compass, carabineer, whistle, magnifying glass, & LED flashlight. (You provide a lighter)

City Bite

- Developed to be carried in the urban & suburban environments, where a person would experience a catastrophe around other people, in buildings, & in a populated area.
- Key chain design that consists of two key rings for car & building keys, flashlight, whistle, 7+ feet of paracord, 2.5" hacksaw knife, wire, needle, safety pin, razor blade, & 3' of alerting ribbon.

Wrist-Bite

• Carried whilst on the wrist. Also known as a *Paracord Bracelet on Steroids*, this convenient bracelet is able to provide the following items in a very compact package:

• 12+' of paracord, 4" hacksaw knife, 2' of wire, a needle, a safety pin, 3' of alerting ribbon, a whistle buckle, 2 fish hooks, 2' of jute twine tinder, metal match, latex water container, 2 nails, dental floss, & a razor blade.

Knife-Bite

• Incorporated into the best survival knife around (Mora), this compact kit can be worn on the belt, on the neck, or attached to a pack.

• Even though a Mora knife the centerpiece of this kit, a small hacksaw blade knife is also included. The saw portion of the small blade is very helpful in making the notch for a bow-drill fire. It can also be used for most mundane tasks, thus conserving the Mora knife for the more important tasks, and thusly not dulling the Mora knife.

• Included as part of this kit is 25' of paracord, 2.5" hacksaw knife, 2' of wire, a needle, a safety pin, 3' of alerting ribbon, a whistle, 2 fish hooks, 2' of jute twine tinder, metal match, latex water

37

container, 2 nails, dental floss, a razor blade, compass, key ring, magnifying glass, & a LED flashlight.

Neck-Bite

- Incorporating both a paracord necklace as well as a Mora knife, this is my favorite way to carry a survival kit. To me it is unobtrusive, easy to access, and the number of useful items are increased due to the design.

- Found within this survival kit is: 30+ feet of paracord, 4" hacksaw knives, 2' lengths of wire, a needle,   safety pin, 3' lengths of alerting ribbon, a whistle buckle, 2 fish hooks, 2' length of jute tinder, a metal match, water container, a compass, key ring, magnifying glass, 2 nails, 4' of dental floss, a razor blade, AA 50 Lumen Nebo Flashlight, a Magnesium Strip with a built-in metal match, & a Mora 511 Carbon Steel Survival Knife.

Belt-Bite

- Our belts are comprised of an actual nylon belt that serves as the base for 100' of true 550 Paracord. If you use the paracord, you'll still have the belt!

- Understandably, the price of the kit is

significantly less than the price of the Belt-Bite. It takes a long time to braid 100' of Paracord. We can show you how, and you will gain not only the experience, but also have a better understanding of how your belt is put together, because you will be the one doing it!

- Included with the *Belt-Bite*: 75+' of Paracord; 4" Hacksaw Knife, 2' of Wire, needle, Safety Pin, 3' lengths of Bright Ribbon, 2 Fish Hooks, 2' of Jute Tinder, Metal Match, Water Container, Magnifying Glass, Mora 511 Knife, 2 Finish Nails, Dental Floss, & a Razor Blade

Stave-Bite

- These hardwood hiking staves are adapted to survival use. The components of our Trilobite are placed inside a cut that is made in the stave, it is secured with Paracord, & this lightweight companion then becomes one of the best friends that you can take along on your outdoor outings.
- Included with the Stave-Bite are the following components: Paracord, Hacksaw Knife, Wire, Needle & Thread, Safety Pin, Bright Ribbon, Whistle, 2 fishhooks, 2' Jute Twine, 1 metal match, 1 water container, 1 compass, 2 finish nails, 4' of Dental Floss, 1 razor blade, 1 Stave.

Youth-Bite

- More than a Kid-Bite, but less than the adult Bites, this youth bite includes items that a young teen may be able to use with some skill. Some practice & becoming familiar is encouraged.
- Included with the Youth-Bite: 5'-8' of Paracord, Hacksaw Knife, Safety Pin, 3-3' Bright Ribbon, 1 whistle, 1 flashlight, 2' Jute, 1 Key Ring, 1 Finish Nail, 4' Floss

Kid-Bite

- Designed for youngsters 3 years of age & older, who are capable of disassembling the Trilobite, but wouldn't know how to use the implements included in the other Trilobites.
- To effectively use the Kid-Bite, there has to be prior training. Our parent study guide is useful for this purpose.
- Included with the Kid-Bite: 5-8" of Paracord, 3 – 3' lengths of surveyor's tape, 1 Whistle, 1 Flashlight, 1 key ring

Tips & Recommendations

- Using brightly colored duct tape, attach a lighter to your Knife-Bite, Neck-Bite, & Wild-Bite, for a quick & easy way to make fire.

- Learn how to braid the Cobra Stitch. When you know this, take your Trilobite apart, look at the pieces, and reassemble the Trilobite.
- Customize your Trilobite. If you've been outdoors, you know what works for you. The items that are included are useful, to be sure, but there are other items that may be useful to you as well. Add these to your kit. Make it work for you, individually. Have fun with it, and make it useful.
- Get a kit for you, your spouse, your parents, as wedding gifts, for your children, your scout troop, & your favorite Aunt!
- Go hiking & camping. Have fun in the outdoors.
- Attend Preparedness Expos. Go to preparedness websites. Read survival books. Especially study the psychology of survival. Then teach it to others. Share your knowledge.

Trilobite (Wild-Bite) Contents

Paracord	12feet
Hacksaw Knife	
Wire	4 feet
Needle	
Safety Pin	3
Bright Ribbon	6 feet
Whistle	
Flashlight	Button LED
Fish Hook	3
Fishing Line	10 feet
Jute	4 feet
Firesteel	
Water Container	
Compass	
Carabiner	
Key Ring	
Finish Nails	3
Dental Floss	4 feet
Razor Blade	
Magnifying Glass	
Lighter (you provide)	

Your Trilobite Quiz:

Why is it a good idea to learn how to do the cobra stitch with paracord?

Where can you go to learn how to do a cobra stitch?

What is the poundage rating of the parachute cord that Dyehard Survival uses in our Trilobite kits?

What is the difference between Stainless Steel and Carbon Steel?

Is it OK to add items to your Trilobite?

Have you started a fire with your metal match?

What copes with the Trilobite that can be used for tinder?

What could this couple have done to create a better outcome for them in their emergency?

Why is it important to wear the Trilobite on your person, and not attach it to a pack?

Have you ever tried to get a flame, or even a spark, from a lighter that has been soaked?

Can you get discounts for purchasing Trilobites in quantity?

Do Trilobites make good gifts?

What percentage of the adult body is water?

What is the core temperature of our body?

Which of these is more important in survival: water, shelter, food

Other Items & Publications provided by Dyehard
Survival

Mora Knives (Carbon & Stainless Steel)

Five-Gallon Bucket Gifts (toilets; water filters;
showers; hand laundry machine; emergency kit; hidden
cache; water filter; and more as time goes on)

Numerous Booklets

Heirloom non-GMO Garden Seeds

The Originals are **EXTINCT!**
Don't let the same thing
Happen to You!!!

Introducing the
TRILOBITE®
Survival Kit Family

'Survival You Can Wear'

Brought to you exclusively by

David Dye
The Preparedness Therapist

Part of the family mission of
Dyehard Survival & Preparedness Academy